Scripture Personified: Binyamin's Brothers and Bil'am

By Shemar Day

Illustrated by Quinn McGowan

DEDICATION

This book is dedicated to above all my Father. May this be used to spread Your Word, Your Message and Your truth.

This book is also dedicated to those who seek to find and share truth.

ACKNOWLEDGMENTS

I want to acknowledge all those who contributed to the making of this publication. From the teachers who often told me I write well, to my friends who participated in Scripture studies with me, to those of you who proofread my work and kept me encouraged and countless others; I thank you.

CONTENTS

Binyamin's Brothers

"I am Ĕl Shaddai. Bear fruit and increase..."
Bereshith/Genesis 35:11

Binyamin, the youngest of his eleven brothers, was renamed by his father after the death of his mother.

He knew his father always seemed over-protective, yet kind.
When his ten brothers went on a journey to buy food, Binyamin had to stay behind.

He did not know why his father selected him to stay or why he seemed so alarmed. All he heard was his father mention something about keeping him from being harmed.

When his brothers arrived in Mitsrayim, the governor spoke very harshly to this group that numbered ten. He claimed they were spies and said they must bring the youngest son in order to prove they were really kin.

The brothers pleaded with the governor, but he did not care. "Nine of you will stay locked in prison until the other one brings the youngest brother here."

Instead, the governor locked all ten of them up and left them confined for three days. When he returned to speak with them, his request had them feeling hopeless, confused and dazed.

"Leave one of your brothers here with me and take food for your households, go. Then, bring your youngest brother to me. If you are not really spying, that's how I'll know."

The men felt full of guilt and worry as they journeyed back. Their anguish was heightened when they realized all their silver had been returned to their sacks.

Shim'on had to stay in Mitsrayim while his brothers brought proof. Returning with Binyamin was the only way to convince the governor that they were telling the truth.

When they had eaten up all the grain, they bought in Mitsrayim, Ya'aqob told them to go back and buy more. Yahudah reminded him, "the governor said we could not return unless Binyamin is with us. We told you that before."

Ya'aqob, their father, immediately told them no. "Yoseph is dead, Shim'on is no more, and now you want Binyamin to go?!"

Reu'bĕn pleaded with his father and asked again. "You may take the lives of my two sons if I myself do not return with Binyamin." "His brother is dead; I'm not sending him with you! If harm shall come to him, I don't know what I'll do."

The scarcity of food was extremely severe in the land, so Ya'aqob sent the remainder of his sons back to Mitsrayim with presents and double the silver in hand.

After the men returned to the house of the ruler with their youngest brother, the overseer of his house invited them to a feast like no other.

The ruler joined the men and asked them questions about their dad. "Is he in good health? Is he still alive?" Then he laid eyes on the youngest lad.

The ruler could not stay around Binyamin; moisture began to fill his eye. He quickly left the men's presence and went to his room to cry.

After washing his face, the ruler returned to eat with the men. Shim'on had been released, so all Ya'aqob's sons were together again.

The sons of Ya'aqob ate wonderfully that night. The next day they were given their things and sent away with the morning light.

Everything seemed great but there was something the men did not know. The ruler and his overseer had conspired against them. For some reason, he did not want Binyamin to go.

They were right outside the city when they were
approached about the contents of their sack.
The ruler's cup was found in Binyamin's possession,
so they all had to go back.

Binyamin's brother pleaded with the ruler to enslave them all. The ruler denied his request and Yahudah was appalled.

He continued to plead for his release with the ruler, but it was of no avail. Yahudah knew he had to explain why Binyamin was so important to their father, so he proceeded to tell him a true tale.

"You know my wife bore me two sons. One went out from me and was torn to pieces; his robe is all that is left. I will not allow Binyamin to journey with you. If harm were to come to him, I will forever feel bereft."

Unable to control his emotions, the ruler sent all the workers from his presence. Then he spoke to the men with humbleness and reverence.

"I am Yoseph, your brother. Is my father still alive?" His brothers stood in silence; they did not know he had survived.

22

Yoseph is their brother whom they sold into Mitsrayim. However, he was neither bitter nor angry. In fact, he praised Elohim.

"I realize that I was sent ahead in order to gain esteem. I was sent ahead so that our whole family could be made great in Mitsrayim."

Binyamin embraced his brother Yoseph and the two wept on each other's neck. Then Yoseph wept with his other brothers and gave each one a peck.

24

Pharaoh was so happy to hear the news of Yoseph's family, he gave them land and invited everyone to stay. It was here, in Mitsrayim, that the descendants of Ya'aqob lived until they were led out by Mosheh.

25

The Story of Bil'am

"Only the word which I speak to you that you do."
Bemidar/Numbers 22:24

The children of Yisra'ĕl came and camped in Moab in the desert plains. The sovereign, Balaq was filled with dread. He did not want them to remain.

The reason Balaq was filled with dread was because he saw that the children of Yisra'ĕl covered the land. So he sent the elders to Bil'am with the divination fee in hand.

"Their number is too great, and their men are too strong! Hurry up and bring Bil'am to me! Hurry up, don't take too long!"

The elders came to Bil'am and he told them to spend the night. He would wait for Yahuah to speak to him and give them word in the morning light.

Yahuah asked about the men and what they desired. He informed Bil'am that the children of Yisra'ĕl are blessed, so he could not be a part of what Balaq conspired.

In the morning Bil'am informed the men that "Yahuah has refused me to go." So the men returned to Balaq and told him Bil'am said no.

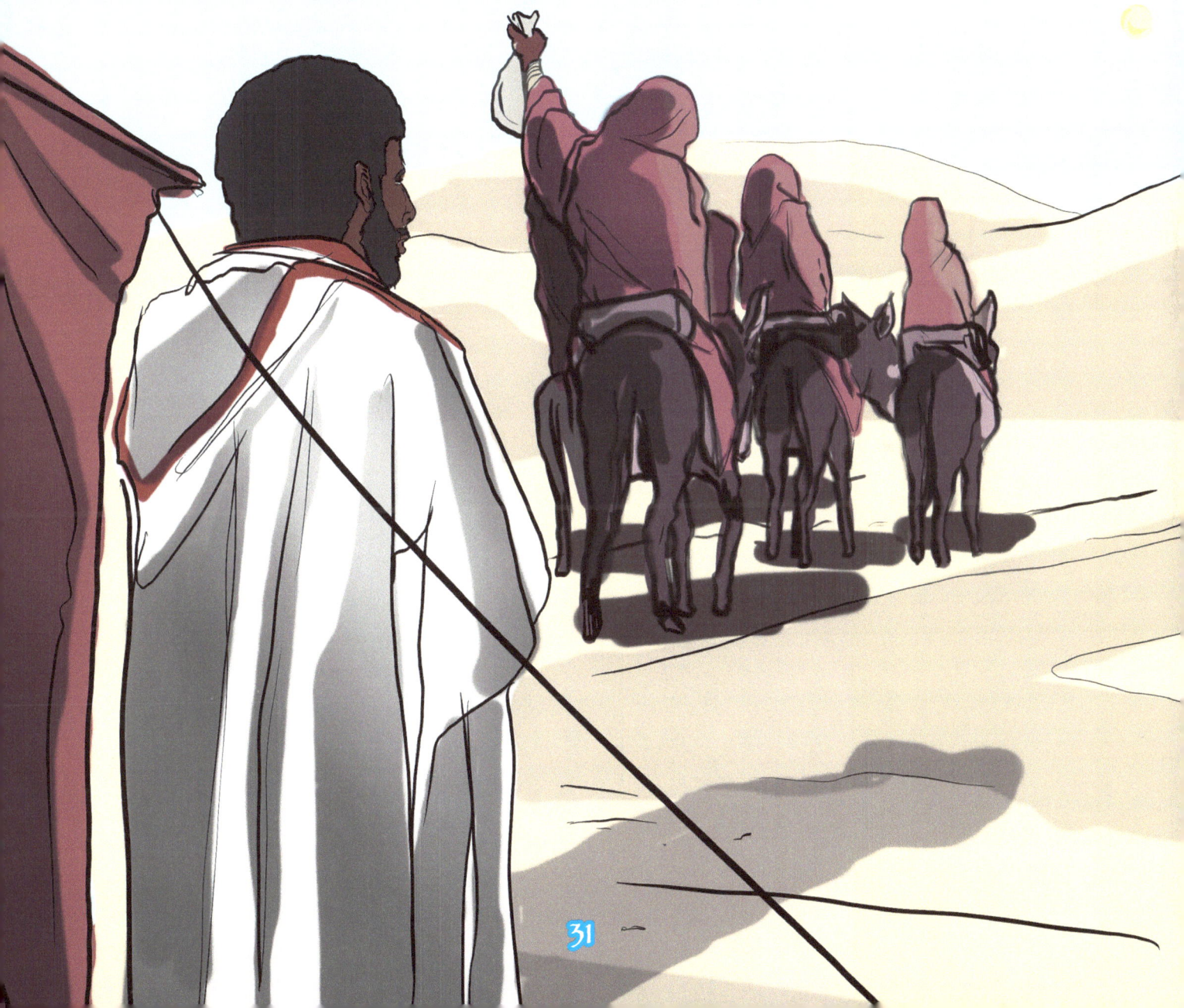

Balaq did not accept it. For he wanted the people cursed. So, he sent another group of men and they were more esteemed than the first.

When the men came to Bil'am he said "Even if Balaq gave me his house filled with silver and gold, I am unable to go beyond the word of Yahuah which I am told."

Despite his words, once again, Bil'am told the men to stay the night. He would wait for Yahuah to speak to him and give them word in the morning light.

Elohim came to Bil'am at night. This is what he said: "If the men come to call, rise and go with them." However, Bil'am chose to do his own thing instead.

The next morning without waiting for the call.
Bil'am saddled his donkey and left with them all.

Elohim's displeasure burned against Bil'am, and he did not have a clue. He ignored the rest of Elohim's words which were "(but) only the word which I speak to you that you do."

While riding, Bil'am's donkey saw a sight that instantly had her floored. In the way of their path was a Messenger of Yahuah standing with a sword.

The donkey did not know what to do. She did not want the sword and Bil'am to collide. So, she avoided the collision by entering a field that was located on the side.

Bil'am was confused. He did not know why his donkey had gone astray. Nevertheless, he beat her and they continued on their way. Then the Messenger stood in a narrow place.

There was a wall on each side and no way of retreating. So the donkey pushed herself against the wall. And for crushing Bil'am's foot, she received another beating.

The Messenger of Yahuah went and stood further in a narrow place where there was no way to turn aside. So the donkey lay down under Bil'am and he used his staff on her hide.

Yahuah opened the donkey's mouth so Bil'am could hear her speak. Her words were very precise. "What have I done to you that you have beaten me thrice?!"

Bil'am replied "because you have mocked me and that's something I cannot allow! If I had a sword in my hand, surely I would've killed you by now!"

"I am your donkey from the beginning until now, I have never done anything like this to you." Bil'am thought back on their time together and realized that everything she said was true.

Just then Yahuah opened Bil'am's eyes. He saw the Messenger of Yahuah standing there with his sword drawn. Bil'am bowed his head, fell on his face and the animosity towards his donkey was all gone.

The Messenger of Yahuah asked, "why have you beaten your donkey three times? Can't you see? I have come out to stand against you because your way has been reckless before Me."

Bil'am apologized to the Messenger, offering to go back even without knowing how much havoc this journey would wreak. However, the Messenger said, "Go with the men" and warned, "but it is only the word that I speak to you that you speak."

After arriving, Balaq wanted to know what had taken Bil'am so long, and why he had not arrived sooner to see what his request was about.

Bil'am stated it did not matter because he was here now, and informed Balaq that he could only say the words that Yahuah had placed in his mouth.

Bil'am instructed Balaq to build seven altars and on each to place a ram and a bull. Then Bil'am went out, spoke to Elohim and delivered his message in full.

"No one could count a quarter of Yisra'ĕl nor of Ya'aqob the dust." Upon hearing the barukah of Yisra'ĕl, Balaq was filled with disgust.

Balaq asked Bil'am to come to another place where only the extremity of the people would show. And even though Yahuah already said they are baruk, Bil'am agreed to go.

Once again Balaq built seven altars and waited for Bil'am to return so he could hear what Elohim would say. "They contain no wickedness or no trouble. Ēl for them is like an ox and they are lifted up like a lion who does not lie down until it devours its prey."

Neither Balaq nor Bil'am wanted to take heed.
Balaq took Bil'am to a third location hoping Yahuah
would curse them indeed.

This third time Bil'am took a change of pace.
Instead of seeking sorcery, the wilderness is where he
set his face.

After the Ruah of Elohim came upon him his eyes
were opened wide. Bil'am was able to hear the
words of Ēl and see the visions of Ēl Shaddai.

After bringing Bil'am to him, Balaq hoped that Yahuah's words could be reversed. However, whomever Yahuah selects to be barak, no man is able to curse.

Before the two men went their separate ways, Bil'am instructed Balaq on what Yisra'ĕl would do to his people in latter days.

46

And while their conversation comes to a close, it seems like Bil'am's words were sincere. However, he had conspired with Balaq against Yisra'ĕl and could not simply disappear.

For you see Yahuah does not like those who interpret omens or practice divination. Elohim sees all these practices as an abomination.

Not only were Bil'am's practices abominable but the words of Yahuah he chose to mock. Although he could not curse Yisra'ĕl, he instructed Balaq on how to set up a stumbling block.

However, Yisra'ĕl turned away, repented and were able to be restored. They captured the women who turned them aside and Bil'am they slew with a sword.

ABOUT THE AUTHOR

Shemar Day is someone who wishes to share truth, engage seekers of truth and display the love of Abba in all future works. Scripture Personified is Shemar Day's first published book series. When not engrossed in reading or writing about Scripture, Shemar enjoys cooking, spending time in nature and teaching.

ABOUT THE ILLUSTRATOR

Quinn McGowan is an artist with over 30 years experience, a member of the Operative Network, the creator artist of Project: Wildfire, the artist responsible for Heroes International (issues one and two), A Tall Order (graphic novel), Luna (issue 2) and is hard at work on the upcoming althistory epic Restless, while also providing the art for Discombobulated with David Walker. He is a Marine, educator, father (to three sons) and husband.

www.ingramcontent.com/pod-product-compliance
Lightning Source LLC
LaVergne TN
LVHW072104070426
835508LV00003B/256